Biblical Counsel on Anger

Joshua Rhoades

Published by Joshua Paul Rhoades, 2024.

While every precaution has been taken in the preparation of this book, the publisher assumes no responsibility for errors or omissions, or for damages resulting from the use of the information contained herein.

BIBLICAL COUNSEL ON ANGER

First edition. September 2, 2024.

Copyright © 2024 Joshua Rhoades.

ISBN: 979-8227629654

Written by Joshua Rhoades.

Also by Joshua Rhoades

Courage Under Fire: David's Stand On The Battlefield
Jonah's Journey: Voices Of Redemption And Lessons In Obedience
The Furnace Of Faith: 12 Principles From The Heat Of Faith
Whispers of Hope: Inspiring Stories of Men's Prayers In Scripture
Frontier Legends: The Oregon Dream
Elijah: A Beacon Of Boldness
HOOK, LINE & SAVIOUR - Faith Reflections from Fishing
Driven By Faith: Motor Racing Inspired Christian Life
30 Day Devotional - Bold and Strong- Coffee Devotions for a
Courageous Christian Walk
Authentic Christianity: The Heart of Old Time Religion
Consider The Ant - God's Tiny Preachers
Flee Fornication: The Plea For Purity
Renewed Hope- How to Find Encouragement in God
Sounding The Call - The Voice of Conviction
The Altar - Where Heaven Meets Earth
The Bible's Battlefields- Timeless Lessons from Ancient Wars
The Sacred Art of Silence - How Silence Speaks in Scripture
Under Fire- The Sanctity of the Traditional Biblical Home
Who Is on the Lord's Side? A Call to Righteousness
What Is Truth? - From Skepticism to Submission
First and Goal- Faith and Football Fundamentals
From Dugout to Devotion- Spiritual Lessons from Baseball
Par for the Course- Faith and Fairways
The Believer's Pace- Tools for Running Life's Marathon

The Immutable Fortress- Security in God's Unchanging Nature
Biblical Bravery
Deer Stands and Devotions: A Hunter's Walk with God
Jesus Knows- Our Hearts, Our Responsibility
Restoration - Setting The Bone
Spiritual 911- God's Word for Life's Emergency's
The Freedom of Forgiveness
The Jezebel Effect - Ancient Manipulations Modern Lessons
The Shout That Stopped The Saviour
The Time Machine Chronicles: Old Testament Characters
Anchored In Truth Exploring The Depths of Psalm 119
Biblical Counsel on Anger

Introduction

Anger is something we all face at some point in our lives. It's a powerful emotion that can lead us to say or do things we later wish we hadn't. But anger, by itself, isn't always wrong—it's a natural reaction to feeling hurt, wronged, or frustrated. The challenge comes in how we handle that anger. If left unchecked, anger can become destructive, tearing apart relationships, causing us to make poor decisions, and pushing us further away from the peace and joy God desires for us. The Bible has a lot to say about anger, offering wisdom that can guide us in managing this emotion in a way that honors God and helps us grow spiritually. "Biblical Counsel on Anger" is a book that dives into what Scripture teaches about anger, providing clear and practical guidance for dealing with it in our daily lives. In this book, we'll explore key Bible passages that speak to the heart of anger—showing us how to be slow to anger, how to distinguish between righteous and sinful anger, and how to respond to situations that trigger our anger with patience, forgiveness, and love. We'll also look at the consequences of letting anger control us and the hope that comes from God's grace when we choose to follow His ways. Whether you struggle with anger yourself, want to help someone else, or simply wish to understand this emotion from a biblical perspective, this book is here to offer you wisdom and tools from God's Word. The Bible is rich with advice on anger, and its teachings are just as relevant today as they were thousands of years ago. As you read, you'll find that by aligning your response to anger with God's guidance, you can break free from the grip of this powerful emotion, live in greater peace, and build healthier, more loving relationships. So, as you journey through "Biblical Counsel on Anger", I encourage you to approach each page with an open heart, ready to learn, grow, and be transformed by the timeless wisdom of Scripture. Let the insights you gain from this book help you manage anger in a way that not only pleases God but also leads to a more peaceful and fulfilling life for you and those around you.

Chapter 1 – The Measured

Proverbs 14:29, "He that is slow to wrath is of great understanding: but he that is hasty of spirit exalteth folly," offers a powerful lesson on the nature of anger and the wisdom of controlling one's temper. The verse highlights the contrast between two types of people: those who are slow to anger and those who are quick to react in anger. Being "slow to wrath" implies a person who takes time to think before responding, someone who exercises patience and seeks to understand the situation fully before allowing their emotions to take over. This person embodies wisdom, showing a deep understanding of how unchecked anger can lead to negative consequences. When we are slow to anger, we give ourselves the opportunity to assess the situation, consider the perspectives of others, and choose a response that is thoughtful and measured. This approach not only prevents unnecessary conflicts but also allows us to maintain relationships and build trust with others. In contrast, the second part of the verse warns against being "hasty of spirit," which refers to those who react quickly and impulsively in anger. This hasty response often leads to actions that are foolish, regrettable, and harmful. The phrase "exalteth folly" suggests that such behavior elevates foolishness, making it more likely that we will make mistakes or cause damage to our relationships and our own well-being. When we are quick to anger, we often act without thinking, saying or doing things that we later regret. This can lead to broken relationships, lost opportunities, and a reputation for being untrustworthy or difficult to deal with. The wisdom in Proverbs 14:29 lies in the recognition that anger, when not controlled, can cloud our judgment and lead us down a path of folly. The verse encourages us to cultivate patience and understanding, to be deliberate in our actions, and to avoid the pitfalls of impulsive anger. By being slow to wrath, we demonstrate maturity, self-control, and a deep understanding of the consequences of our actions. This measured approach to anger is not about suppressing our emotions or pretending that we don't feel angry; rather, it's about taking the time to process our emotions and respond in a way that is constructive rather than destructive. The verse also suggests that understanding, or wisdom, comes from being slow to anger. When we take the time to understand a situation fully, we are better equipped to respond in a way that is appropriate and effective. This understanding allows us to see the bigger picture, to consider the long-term consequences of our actions, and to choose a path that leads to peace and reconciliation rather than conflict and division. On the other hand, when we are hasty in our spirit, we often miss important details, overlook the feelings and perspectives of others, and make decisions that we later regret. The folly that is exalted in these moments can take many forms: harsh words that cannot be taken back, rash decisions that have lasting consequences, or actions that damage our relationships and our reputation. In contrast, those who are slow to anger are often seen as wise, trustworthy, and reliable. They are the people others turn to for guidance and support, knowing that they will respond with thoughtfulness and care. This type of person builds strong, healthy relationships, fosters a sense of trust and respect, and creates an environment where others feel safe and valued. The verse also highlights the importance of self-control in managing our emotions. Being slow to anger requires a conscious effort to control our impulses and to resist the urge to react immediately. It involves taking a step back, breathing deeply, and giving ourselves the space to think before we act. This self-control is a sign of strength, not weakness, and it is a key component of wisdom. Those who lack this self-control, who are hasty in their spirit, often find themselves in situations where their anger leads them into trouble. They may struggle with broken relationships, unresolved conflicts, and a reputation for being difficult or volatile. The folly that they exalt through their quick-tempered reactions can have lasting effects on their lives and the lives of those around them. The wisdom of Proverbs 14:29 is timeless and universally applicable. Whether we are dealing with family, friends, colleagues, or strangers, the principle of being slow to anger can help us navigate difficult situations with grace and wisdom. It teaches us the value of patience, the importance of understanding, and the power of self-control. By applying this verse to our lives, we can avoid the pitfalls of impulsive anger and instead cultivate a spirit of peace, understanding, and wisdom. This verse also encourages us to reflect on our own behavior and to recognize the areas where we may need to grow. Are we quick to anger, reacting impulsively to situations without fully understanding them? Do we exalt folly through our hasty words and actions? Or do we take the time to be slow to wrath, seeking understanding and wisdom in our responses? By examining our own hearts and actions in light of this verse, we can identify the areas where we need to improve and make a conscious effort to cultivate patience and self-control. The benefits of being slow to anger are numerous. Not only does it help us avoid the negative consequences of hasty reactions, but it also allows us to build stronger, healthier relationships. When we are patient and understanding, we create an environment where others feel safe to express themselves, knowing that we will respond with kindness and wisdom. This type of environment fosters trust, respect, and mutual understanding, leading to deeper and more meaningful connections with others. Additionally, being slow to anger can improve our own well-being. Anger, when not managed well, can be harmful to our physical and mental health. It can lead to stress, anxiety, and even physical ailments such as high blood pressure and heart disease. By practicing patience and self-control, we can reduce the negative impact of anger on our health and improve our overall sense of peace and well-being. The wisdom of Proverbs 14:29 also extends beyond our personal lives and into our communities and society as a whole. When individuals practice being slow to anger, it contributes to a more peaceful and harmonious society. It reduces the likelihood of conflicts escalating into violence, fosters a culture of understanding and respect, and promotes the common good. In a world where anger and conflict often seem to be the norm, the wisdom of being slow to anger is more important than ever. By embodying this principle in our own lives, we can set an example for others and contribute to a more peaceful and just world. In conclusion, Proverbs 14:29 offers profound wisdom on the nature of anger and the importance of being measured, patient, and understanding in our responses. It contrasts the wisdom of being slow to anger with the folly of being quick-tempered, highlighting the benefits of self-control and the dangers of impulsive reactions. This verse encourages us to cultivate patience, seek understanding, and practice self-control in all our interactions. By doing so, we can avoid the pitfalls of anger, build stronger relationships, and contribute to a more peaceful and harmonious world. The wisdom of this verse is timeless and universally applicable, offering valuable guidance for navigating the challenges of life with grace and wisdom. Whether we are dealing with personal conflicts, professional challenges, or societal issues, the principle of being slow to anger can help us respond in a way that is thoughtful, measured, and constructive. By applying the wisdom of Proverbs 14:29 to our lives, we can become people of great understanding, known for our patience, wisdom, and self-control. This approach not only benefits us and those around us, but it also reflects the character of God, who is described in the Bible as "merciful and gracious, slow to anger, and plenteous in mercy" (Psalm 103:8). In a world that often values quick reactions and impulsive decisions, the wisdom of being slow to anger stands out as a powerful and transformative principle. It challenges us to be more thoughtful, more understanding, and more patient in all our interactions, and it offers the promise of a life marked by peace, wisdom, and fulfillment. Proverbs 14:29 reminds us that true wisdom lies not in the ability to react quickly, but in the ability to respond thoughtfully, with patience and understanding. By embracing this wisdom, we can navigate the challenges of life with grace and become people of great understanding, whose lives are marked by peace, wisdom, and the absence of folly.

Chapter 2 – The Mild

Proverbs 15:1, "A soft answer turneth away wrath: but grievous words stir up anger," is a verse that speaks to the power of our words and how they can either calm a situation or make it worse. This verse emphasizes the importance of responding gently and kindly, especially when confronted with anger or conflict. A "soft answer" refers to a gentle, calm, and measured response. It suggests that when someone is angry or upset, replying with kindness and understanding can help to deescalate the situation and bring peace. In contrast, "grievous words" are harsh, hurtful, or confrontational words that can provoke further anger and escalate the conflict. The wisdom in this verse lies in the recognition that our words have the power to either calm or inflame a situation. When we choose to respond with a soft answer, we are taking control of the situation, not allowing anger to dictate our actions. Instead, we are choosing to respond with wisdom and grace, seeking to bring peace and understanding. This approach not only helps to diffuse anger but also fosters better communication and stronger relationships. On the other hand, when we respond with grievous words, we are likely to stir up more anger and make the situation worse. Harsh words can hurt others, create resentment, and lead to a breakdown in communication. They can turn a simple disagreement into a full-blown argument, causing lasting damage to relationships. Proverbs 15:1 teaches us that the way we speak to others, especially in moments of tension or conflict, can have a profound impact on the outcome of the situation. By choosing to respond with a soft answer, we can turn away wrath and create an environment where understanding and reconciliation are possible. This verse is not just about avoiding conflict but about actively promoting peace. It encourages us to be mindful of our words and to recognize the power they hold. A soft answer can soothe anger, calm tensions, and create a space for constructive dialogue. It can help to prevent misunderstandings, reduce hostility, and build trust. When we respond with kindness, even in the face of anger, we are demonstrating strength and wisdom. We are showing that we value the relationship more than winning an argument or proving a point. This approach requires self-control and humility, but the rewards are great. A soft answer can turn a potentially explosive situation into an opportunity for growth and deeper understanding. In contrast, grievous words can stir up anger and lead to further conflict. They can create a cycle of hostility, where each person responds to the other's anger with more anger, escalating the situation and causing more harm. This cycle can be difficult to break and can lead to lasting damage to relationships. Proverbs 15:1 reminds us that we have the power to choose how we respond to anger. We can choose to respond with a soft answer, turning away wrath and promoting peace, or we can choose to respond with grievous words, stirring up more anger and conflict. The choice is ours, and the consequences of our choice can have a lasting impact on our relationships and our lives. This verse also highlights the importance of listening before we speak. When we take the time to listen and understand the other person's perspective, we are more likely to respond with a soft answer. Listening shows that we value the other person and their feelings, and it allows us to respond in a way that is thoughtful and considerate. By contrast, when we respond with grievous words, it often indicates that we have not taken the time to listen and understand the other person's perspective. Instead, we are reacting out of our own anger or frustration, without considering the impact of our words. This reactive approach can lead to misunderstandings and further conflict. The wisdom in Proverbs 15:1 lies in its call to be intentional about our words and our responses. It encourages us to be proactive in seeking peace, rather than reactive in responding to anger. A soft answer is a powerful tool for diffusing anger and promoting understanding, while grievous words can only serve to escalate the situation. In our daily lives, we are often faced with situations where our words can either calm or inflame a situation. Whether it is in our relationships with family, friends, colleagues, or strangers, the principle of Proverbs 15:1 can help us navigate these situations with wisdom and grace. By choosing to respond with a soft answer, we can turn away wrath and create an environment where positive communication and understanding can flourish. This verse also teaches us about the importance of self-control. It takes self-control to respond with a soft answer, especially when we are feeling angry or hurt. It is easy to react with harsh words when we feel attacked or misunderstood, but Proverbs 15:1 encourages us to rise above these impulses and choose a response that promotes peace and understanding. Self-control is a key aspect of wisdom, and it is essential for maintaining healthy relationships. When we exercise self-control in our words and actions, we are better able to manage our emotions and respond in a way that is constructive rather than destructive. Proverbs 15:1 reminds us that a soft answer is not a sign of weakness, but of strength and wisdom. It shows that we are in control of our emotions and that we are committed to promoting peace and understanding in our relationships. In contrast, grievous words often reflect a lack of self-control and can lead to further conflict and hurt. The verse also highlights the importance of humility. Responding with a soft answer requires humility, as it often means putting the other person's feelings and needs ahead of our own desire to be right or to have the last word. Humility allows us to respond with kindness and understanding, even when we feel wronged or misunderstood. Proverbs 15:1 encourages us to approach conflict with a spirit of humility, recognizing that our words have the power to either heal or harm. When we respond with humility and a soft answer, we are more likely to turn away wrath and promote reconciliation. This approach fosters a sense of mutual respect and understanding, which is essential for healthy and lasting relationships. In contrast, responding with grievous words often reflects pride and a desire to assert our own position, regardless of the impact on the other person. This approach can lead to increased conflict and resentment, making it difficult to resolve the situation and move forward. Proverbs 15:1 teaches us that our words matter, and that the way we choose to respond to anger can have a profound impact on our relationships and our lives. By choosing to respond with a soft answer, we can turn away wrath and promote peace, understanding, and reconciliation. This verse encourages us to be intentional about our words, to exercise self-control, and to approach conflict with humility. In doing so, we can build stronger, healthier relationships and create a more peaceful and harmonious environment in our lives. The wisdom of Proverbs 15:1 is timeless and universally applicable. Whether we are dealing with personal conflicts, professional challenges, or everyday interactions, the principle of responding with a soft answer can help us navigate these situations with grace and wisdom. It reminds us that we have the power to choose how we respond to anger, and that our words can either build up or tear down. By embracing the wisdom of Proverbs 15:1, we can become peacemakers in our relationships and in the world around us. We can choose to respond with a soft answer, turning away wrath and promoting understanding, or we can choose to respond with grievous words, stirring up anger and conflict. The choice is ours, and the consequences of our choice can have a lasting impact on our lives and the lives of those around us. In conclusion, Proverbs 15:1 offers profound wisdom on the power of our words and the importance of responding to anger with a soft answer. It encourages us to be mindful of our words, to exercise self-control, and to approach conflict with humility. By doing so, we can turn away wrath, promote peace, and build stronger, healthier relationships. The wisdom of this verse is a valuable guide for navigating the challenges of life with grace and understanding, and it reminds us that our words have the power to either calm or inflame a situation. By choosing to respond with a soft answer, we can create a more peaceful and harmonious environment in our lives and in the lives of those around us.

Chapter 3 – The Mastery

Proverbs 16:32, "He that is slow to anger is better than the mighty; and he that ruleth his spirit than he that taketh a city," offers a profound insight into the nature of true strength and mastery. This verse contrasts two types of power: the physical might needed to conquer a city and the inner strength required to control one's temper. While society often celebrates the external displays of power, such as the ability to lead armies or achieve great victories, this verse suggests that the ability to govern oneself, especially in the face of anger, is a higher and more admirable form of strength. Mastery over one's temper is not just a sign of self-control but also of deep understanding and wisdom. Being "slow to anger" involves the ability to pause, reflect, and choose a measured response rather than reacting impulsively out of emotion. This kind of mastery requires patience, discipline, and a commitment to personal growth. It is easy to lash out when provoked, to let anger take over and dictate our actions, but it takes true strength to remain calm and composed, even in situations that might otherwise lead to frustration or rage. The verse implies that ruling one's spirit, or mastering one's emotions, is a greater achievement than the conquest of a city. In ancient times, the ability to take a city was seen as the ultimate demonstration of power and success. It required strategic planning, military strength, and the ability to lead and inspire others. However, Proverbs 16:32 challenges this notion by elevating the mastery of one's temper above even the greatest military victories. This comparison highlights the importance of self-control and emotional intelligence in living a successful and fulfilling life. The ability to control one's anger is not just about avoiding conflict or maintaining peace, although those are certainly important outcomes. It is also about the personal integrity and strength that come from mastering one's own emotions. When we control our temper, we demonstrate that we are not slaves to our emotions but rather capable of thoughtful and deliberate action. This self-mastery is a key component of wisdom and maturity. It allows us to navigate the challenges of life with grace and poise, rather than being swept away by the tides of emotion. Moreover, being slow to anger and ruling one's spirit are essential qualities for effective leadership. A leader who can control their emotions is better equipped to make sound decisions, build strong relationships, and inspire confidence in others. In contrast, a leader who is quick to anger may alienate those they lead, make rash decisions, and ultimately undermine their own authority. Proverbs 16:32 reminds us that true leadership begins with self-leadership. To lead others effectively, we must first be able to lead ourselves, and that includes mastering our emotions. The verse also speaks to the broader concept of personal responsibility. We are each responsible for our own actions and reactions, regardless of the circumstances we find ourselves in. While it is easy to blame others or external factors for our anger, Proverbs 16:32 suggests that we have the power to choose how we respond. By being slow to anger and ruling our spirit, we take control of our own lives and refuse to be victims of circumstance. This personal responsibility is empowering and can lead to greater peace and fulfillment in life. Furthermore, the verse highlights the long-term benefits of mastering one's temper. While anger may provide a temporary release of frustration, it often leads to negative consequences, such as damaged relationships, regret, and a loss of respect from others. On the other hand, those who are slow to anger and rule their spirit are likely to experience more positive outcomes, such as stronger relationships, greater respect from others, and a more peaceful and fulfilling life. Mastering one's temper is not just about avoiding the negative consequences of anger but also about creating the conditions for long-term success and happiness. In addition, Proverbs 16:32 encourages us to see challenges as opportunities for growth. Every time we are faced with a situation that could provoke anger, we have the chance to practice self-mastery and develop our inner strength. Rather than seeing these situations as annoyances or obstacles, we can view them as opportunities to become better versions of ourselves. This mindset shift can transform the way we approach life and help us cultivate a sense of inner peace and resilience. The verse also reminds us of the importance of humility. Mastering one's temper requires a recognition that we are not perfect and that we have room to grow. It involves acknowledging our weaknesses and making a conscious effort to improve. This humility is essential for personal growth and development. It allows us to learn from our mistakes, seek guidance from others, and remain open to new perspectives. By cultivating humility, we can become more effective at ruling our spirit and mastering our emotions. Moreover, Proverbs 16:32 challenges us to redefine our understanding of strength. In a world that often equates strength with physical power, dominance, or control over others, this verse suggests that true strength lies in self-mastery. It is not about imposing our will on others but about governing ourselves with wisdom and grace. This redefinition of strength can have a profound impact on the way we live our lives and interact with others. It encourages us to focus on developing our inner qualities, such as patience, compassion, and self-control, rather than seeking external validation or dominance. In addition to its personal implications, Proverbs 16:32 has broader social and cultural significance. In a world that is often marked by conflict, aggression, and a lack of emotional restraint, the wisdom of this verse offers a path to greater peace and harmony. By cultivating the qualities of patience, self-control, and humility, we can contribute to a more peaceful and just society. We can become role models for others, demonstrating that true strength lies not in the ability to dominate or control others, but in the ability to govern ourselves. This approach to life can help to break the cycles of anger and violence that so often plague our communities and lead to more constructive and positive outcomes. The verse also has spiritual significance, as it aligns with the broader teachings of the Bible on the importance of self-control and humility. Throughout the Scriptures, we are encouraged to cultivate these qualities as part of our spiritual growth and development. By mastering our temper and ruling our spirit, we are better able to live in accordance with God's will and reflect His character in our lives. This spiritual dimension adds depth and meaning to the practice of self-mastery, reminding us that it is not just about personal success but about living a life that honors God and serves others. In conclusion, Proverbs 16:32 offers profound wisdom on the nature of true strength and mastery. It challenges us to redefine our understanding of strength, focusing not on external displays of power but on the inner qualities of patience, self-control, and humility. By being slow to anger and ruling our spirit, we demonstrate true mastery over ourselves and create the conditions for long-term success, happiness, and fulfillment. This verse encourages us to take personal responsibility for our actions, to see challenges as opportunities for growth, and to cultivate the qualities that lead to a more peaceful and harmonious life. The wisdom of Proverbs 16:32 is timeless and universally applicable, offering valuable guidance for navigating the challenges of life with grace and wisdom. Whether in our personal lives, our relationships, or our leadership roles, the principles of self-mastery and emotional intelligence are essential for living a successful and fulfilling life. By embracing the teachings of this verse, we can become people of true strength, who lead ourselves and others with wisdom, grace, and integrity. This mastery over our temper is not just about avoiding conflict or maintaining peace, but about cultivating the inner strength and wisdom that lead to a life of true success and fulfillment. In a world that often values external displays of power and success, Proverbs 16:32 reminds us that the greatest achievements are those that come from within, from the mastery of our own spirit and the cultivation of the qualities that lead to a life of peace, joy, and harmony. By focusing on this inner strength, we can create a life that is not only successful by external standards but also deeply fulfilling and aligned with our highest values and aspirations. The wisdom of Proverbs 16:32 is a powerful reminder of the importance of self-mastery in living a life of true strength, success, and fulfillment.

Chapter 4 – The Moderation

Ephesians 4:26, "Be ye angry, and sin not: let not the sun go down upon your wrath," offers a powerful and practical teaching about how to handle anger in a way that aligns with wisdom and righteousness. The verse begins with an acknowledgment of a fundamental truth about human nature: anger is a natural emotion that we all experience. It is not the emotion of anger itself that is problematic but how we respond to it and what we allow it to lead us to do. The verse commands us to "be ye angry," recognizing that anger can arise for various reasons, some of which may be justified, such as when we encounter injustice, wrongdoing, or situations that violate our moral values. However, the verse immediately follows this acknowledgment with a crucial directive: "and sin not." This phrase calls for moderation in our anger, urging us to control it so that it does not lead us into sinful behavior. Anger, if not managed properly, can quickly escalate into actions or words that harm others or ourselves, leading to sin. This could manifest in various forms such as harsh words, resentment, violence, or holding grudges. The verse advises us to feel the anger but not let it dominate us or push us into actions that are contrary to God's will and teachings. This moderation in anger is key to living a life that is both emotionally healthy and spiritually aligned with Christian values. The second part of the verse, "let not the sun go down upon your wrath," emphasizes the importance of resolving anger quickly. This phrase suggests that while anger may be a natural and sometimes necessary response to certain situations, it should not be allowed to linger or fester. Holding onto anger for an extended period can lead to bitterness, resentment, and a hardened heart, all of which can damage relationships and our own well-being. By advising us not to let the sun go down on our wrath, the verse encourages us to seek resolution and reconciliation before the day ends. This could mean addressing the source of our anger directly, forgiving those who have wronged us, or letting go of the offense to find peace within ourselves. The wisdom in this teaching lies in the recognition that unresolved anger can be corrosive, both to our relationships with others and to our own spiritual and emotional health. When we allow anger to persist, it can take root in our hearts, leading to a cycle of negativity and destructive behavior. This can affect our interactions with others, our outlook on life, and even our physical health. By resolving anger quickly, we prevent it from taking control and leading us down a path of sin and destruction. Moreover, the verse teaches us about the importance of emotional maturity and self-control. To "be ye angry, and sin not" requires a high level of self-awareness and discipline. It involves recognizing when we are angry, understanding why we feel that way, and making a conscious decision to respond in a way that is constructive rather than destructive. This is not always easy, especially in the heat of the moment, but it is a vital skill for living a life that honors God and fosters healthy relationships. Emotional maturity means being able to acknowledge our feelings without letting them dictate our actions. It means taking a step back, reflecting on the situation, and choosing a response that aligns with our values and the teachings of the Bible. The verse also highlights the importance of forgiveness and letting go. By advising us not to let the sun go down on our wrath, it implicitly encourages us to forgive those who have wronged us and to release any lingering anger before it turns into something more harmful. Forgiveness is a central theme in Christian teaching, and it is closely tied to the idea of resolving anger quickly. When we forgive, we are not only releasing the other person from the burden of their offense, but we are also freeing ourselves from the weight of anger and resentment. This act of forgiveness allows us to move forward without carrying the emotional baggage that can hinder our spiritual growth and well-being. In addition to personal growth, this verse has important implications for our relationships with others. Anger, if not managed well, can lead to conflicts and misunderstandings that strain or even break relationships. By being mindful of how we handle anger, we can prevent unnecessary conflicts and promote reconciliation and harmony.

This is especially important in close relationships, such as those with family members, friends, or colleagues, where unresolved anger can have lasting negative effects. Ephesians 4:26 encourages us to take responsibility for our emotions and our actions, recognizing that the way we handle anger can either build up or tear down our relationships. The verse also speaks to the importance of living in the present and not carrying the burdens of the past into the future. By advising us to resolve our anger before the sun goes down, it encourages us to deal with issues as they arise rather than letting them linger and grow. This approach to life promotes a sense of peace and well-being, as we are not weighed down by unresolved issues or lingering resentment. It also aligns with the broader biblical teaching of living each day fully and not worrying about tomorrow, as reflected in verses like Matthew 6:34, which says, "Take therefore no thought for the morrow: for the morrow shall take thought for the things of itself." This mindset helps us to live more fully in the present, with a clear mind and a peaceful heart. Furthermore, this verse calls us to be peacemakers in our own lives and in the lives of others. By managing our anger and resolving conflicts quickly, we can create an environment of peace and harmony. This is in line with the teachings of Jesus, who said, "Blessed are the peacemakers: for they shall be called the children of God" (Matthew 5:9). Being a peacemaker requires us to be proactive in addressing issues, seeking reconciliation, and promoting understanding and forgiveness. It means not only controlling our own anger but also helping others to manage theirs, fostering an environment where peace and love can thrive. The verse also encourages us to trust in God's justice rather than seeking our own vengeance when we are wronged. By resolving our anger quickly, we are essentially placing the situation in God's hands, trusting that He will bring justice in His own time and way. This aligns with Romans 12:19, which says, "Dearly beloved, avenge not yourselves, but rather give place unto wrath: for it is written, Vengeance is mine; I will repay, saith the Lord." This trust in God's justice allows us to let go of anger and resentment, knowing that we do not need to carry the burden of revenge. Instead, we can focus on living in accordance with God's will, promoting peace and forgiveness in our lives. Additionally, the verse calls us to be examples of Christ-like behavior in how we handle anger. Jesus Himself displayed righteous anger at times, such as when He cleansed the temple of the money changers, but He never let His anger lead to sin. He always acted in a way that was consistent with His mission of love, justice, and redemption. Ephesians 4:26 encourages us to follow His example, managing our anger in a way that is aligned with our faith and values. This means being mindful of how our actions reflect on our faith and on the message of the Gospel. When we handle anger with grace and moderation, we demonstrate the transformative power of God's love in our lives. In conclusion, Ephesians 4:26 provides profound guidance on how to manage anger in a way that is both practical and spiritually aligned. It acknowledges that anger is a natural part of life but calls us to handle it with moderation, ensuring that it does not lead us into sin. By advising us not to let the sun go down on our wrath, the verse encourages us to resolve anger quickly, promoting emotional and spiritual well-being. This teaching fosters emotional maturity, self-control, and forgiveness, which are essential for healthy relationships and personal growth. The verse also aligns with the broader biblical themes of peace, forgiveness, and trust in God's justice. By embracing the wisdom of Ephesians 4:26, we can navigate the challenges of life with grace and live in a way that reflects the love and peace of Christ. Whether in our personal lives, our relationships, or our broader communities, the principles of moderation in anger and quick resolution of conflicts are key to living a life that honors God and promotes harmony. This verse is a timeless reminder of the importance of managing our emotions in a way that fosters peace, love, and understanding in our lives and in the lives of those around us.

Chapter 5 – The Mindful

James 1:19-20, "Wherefore, my beloved brethren, let every man be swift to hear, slow to speak, slow to wrath: For the wrath of man worketh not the righteousness of God," is a verse that speaks profoundly to the importance of mindfulness in our everyday interactions and in how we manage our emotions, particularly anger. These two verses offer a practical and spiritual guide for living a life that is both wise and aligned with God's will. The advice begins with the call to be "swift to hear," which emphasizes the value of listening carefully and attentively before reacting or speaking. In a world where we are often quick to voice our opinions or defend our positions, this directive encourages us to take a step back and truly listen to what others are saying. Listening is not just about hearing words; it involves understanding the underlying emotions, intentions, and perspectives of others. Being swift to hear means being present in the moment, fully engaging with the person speaking, and seeking to understand their point of view before forming a response. This practice of active listening can prevent misunderstandings, build stronger relationships, and foster a deeper sense of empathy and connection with others. It shows that we value the thoughts and feelings of those around us, and it can often diffuse tension before it escalates into conflict. Following the command to be swift to hear, the verse instructs us to be "slow to speak." This advice underscores the importance of carefully considering our words before we speak. Words have incredible power; they can build up or tear down, heal or hurt, encourage or discourage. By being slow to speak, we give ourselves the time to reflect on what we are about to say and to ensure that our words are thoughtful, kind, and constructive. This mindfulness in speaking can help us avoid saying things in anger or frustration that we might later regret. It also allows us to respond in ways that are more aligned with our values and with the teachings of Christ. When we take the time to think before we speak, we are more likely to choose words that promote peace, understanding, and reconciliation rather than words that fuel conflict or misunderstanding. The third part of the verse, "slow to wrath," is a call to control our tempers and to be mindful of how we respond to situations that provoke anger. Anger is a natural human emotion, but it can be destructive if not managed properly. When we are quick to anger, we often react impulsively, without fully considering the consequences of our actions or words. Being slow to wrath means exercising patience and self-control, allowing ourselves time to cool down and think rationally before responding. This approach can prevent us from acting in ways that we might later regret and helps us to maintain our relationships and our integrity. It is important to note that being slow to wrath does not mean suppressing our emotions or avoiding difficult conversations; rather, it means approaching these situations with a calm and measured demeanor, ensuring that our actions and words are in line with God's will and with the principles of love, grace, and forgiveness. The second verse, "For the wrath of man worketh not the righteousness of God," provides the rationale for why we should be mindful in our listening, speaking, and in controlling our anger. This verse reminds us that human anger, when not controlled, does not produce the kind of righteousness that God desires from us. Righteousness, in this context, refers to living in a way that is just, virtuous, and in accordance with God's commands. When we allow our anger to dictate our actions, we are often led away from righteousness and into behaviors that are harmful, both to ourselves and to others. Anger can cloud our judgment, lead us to speak or act in ways that are unkind or unjust, and ultimately damage our relationships and our witness as followers of Christ. By being mindful of our anger and seeking to control it, we are better able to live in a way that reflects God's righteousness and love. The wisdom in James 1:19-20 is timeless and universally applicable. Whether we are dealing with personal relationships, professional challenges, or broader societal issues, the principles of being swift to hear, slow to speak, and slow to wrath can help us navigate these situations with wisdom and grace. In our personal lives, this mindfulness can lead to stronger, healthier relationships, as we become better listeners, more thoughtful communicators, and more patient and understanding in our interactions with others. In the workplace, these principles can help us manage conflicts, make better decisions, and foster a more collaborative and supportive environment. On a broader societal level, the teachings of James 1:19-20 encourage us to approach disagreements and conflicts with a spirit of humility and openness, seeking to understand before we judge and to respond with love rather than anger. This approach can lead to more constructive dialogues, greater empathy and understanding, and a more just and compassionate society. Furthermore, the verse calls us to examine our own hearts and motivations. It challenges us to consider whether our actions and words are driven by anger or by a genuine desire to do what is right in God's eyes. When we are mindful of our emotions and take the time to listen, think, and reflect, we are more likely to act in ways that are aligned with God's will and that promote His righteousness in the world. This self-examination is crucial for our spiritual growth and for living a life that honors God. Additionally, the verse highlights the importance of humility in our interactions with others. Being swift to hear and slow to speak requires us to set aside our own ego and to prioritize the needs and perspectives of others. It means being willing to listen and learn, even when we think we already know the answer or when we feel justified in our anger. This humility is a key aspect of living a life that is pleasing to God and that reflects His love and grace to those around us. By approaching our interactions with a humble and open heart, we are better able to build bridges of understanding and to create a more peaceful and harmonious world. Moreover, the verse speaks to the importance of self-control, particularly in how we manage our anger. Anger is a powerful emotion, and it can be difficult to control, especially in the heat of the moment. However, James 1:19-20 calls us to be mindful of our anger and to exercise self-control in how we respond to it. This self-control is not about suppressing our emotions but about channeling them in a way that is constructive and aligned with God's will. It means taking the time to cool down, to pray, and to seek God's guidance before we respond. By doing so, we can ensure that our actions are driven by love, wisdom, and a desire to promote righteousness, rather than by anger or a desire for revenge. In addition to its practical wisdom, James 1:19-20 also offers profound spiritual guidance. The verse reminds us that our ultimate goal as followers of Christ is to live in a way that reflects God's righteousness. This means not only avoiding sinful behaviors but also actively seeking to do what is right in God's eyes. By being mindful of our emotions and our actions, we can ensure that we are living in a way that is pleasing to God and that promotes His kingdom on earth. This mindfulness is a key aspect of our spiritual journey, helping us to grow in our faith and to become more like Christ in our thoughts, words, and actions. The verse also encourages us to trust in God's wisdom and guidance. When we are swift to hear, slow to speak, and slow to wrath, we are acknowledging that we do not have all the answers and that we need God's help to navigate the challenges of life. This trust in God's wisdom allows us to approach life with a sense of peace and confidence, knowing that He is guiding us and that He will provide the strength and wisdom we need to do what is right. It also frees us from the burden of trying to control everything ourselves, allowing us to rest in the assurance that God is in control and that He is working all things for our good. In conclusion, James 1:19-20 offers profound and practical guidance for living a life that is both mindful and aligned with God's will. The verse calls us to be swift to hear, slow to speak, and slow to wrath, reminding us that our words and actions have the power to either promote righteousness or to lead us away from it. By being mindful of our emotions and our responses, we can ensure that we are living in a way that reflects God's love, wisdom, and righteousness. This mindfulness is essential for our spiritual growth, our relationships with others, and our ability to navigate the challenges of life with grace and wisdom. Whether in our personal lives, our professional interactions, or our broader societal engagements, the principles of James 1:19-20 can help us to live in a way that honors God and that promotes His kingdom on earth. By embracing the teachings of this verse, we can become more effective listeners, more thoughtful communicators, and more patient and understanding in our interactions with others. We can also ensure that our actions are driven by a desire to do what is right in God's eyes, rather than by anger or impulsive reactions. In doing so, we can live a life that is both pleasing to God and a blessing to those around us, reflecting His love, grace, and righteousness in all that we do. The wisdom of James 1:19-20 is timeless and universally applicable, offering valuable guidance for living a life that is mindful, righteous, and aligned with God's will.

Chapter 6 – The Merciful

Proverbs 19:11, "The discretion of a man deferreth his anger; and it is his glory to pass over a transgression," presents a powerful message about the virtue of mercy and the strength it takes to overlook offenses, guiding us toward a life of wisdom, peace, and maturity. At its core, this verse emphasizes the importance of discretion—the ability to judge what is right and wise in a given situation—particularly when it comes to managing anger. Discretion, in this context, is about making thoughtful and deliberate choices rather than reacting impulsively to the actions of others. When we encounter situations that provoke anger, whether it's a harsh word, an unfair accusation, or any kind of offense, our natural instinct might be to retaliate or express our frustration immediately. However, this verse advises us to defer our anger, meaning to delay or put off our immediate emotional response. This act of deferral is not a sign of weakness, but of immense strength and self-control. It shows that we are not ruled by our emotions, but instead, we have the ability to pause, reflect, and decide how best to respond in a way that aligns with our values and the teachings of the Bible. The verse goes further to suggest that it is "glory"—a noble and admirable quality—to pass over a transgression, to let go of the offense without seeking revenge or holding a grudge. In a world where reacting in anger is often seen as justified or even necessary, this call to mercy stands out as a path of true greatness and inner strength.

Being merciful and choosing to overlook an offense is not about ignoring wrongdoing or allowing ourselves to be mistreated. Rather, it is about recognizing that not every situation requires a strong emotional reaction and that sometimes, the most powerful response is one of patience and forgiveness. This approach allows us to rise above the immediate hurt or irritation and focus on the bigger picture—our long-term peace, our relationships, and our spiritual growth. When we defer our anger, we give ourselves the opportunity to consider the consequences of our actions and to choose a path that leads to healing and reconciliation rather than further conflict. It is in this space of reflection that true wisdom is exercised, as we align our actions with the principles of love, grace, and mercy that are central to the Christian faith.

Furthermore, the glory of passing over a transgression is found in the peace it brings to our own hearts and the relationships we value. When we choose not to react in anger, we prevent the situation from escalating into something more damaging. We also protect ourselves from the negative effects of holding onto anger, such as bitterness, resentment, and a loss of inner peace. By letting go of the offense and forgiving the person who wronged us, we free ourselves from the burden of carrying that anger with us. This act of mercy is not only beneficial to the person we forgive but also to ourselves, as it allows us to maintain a sense of calm and well-being, even in the face of provocation. Over time, this practice of mercy can transform our relationships, making them stronger and more resilient because they are not easily shaken by misunderstandings or offenses.

In addition, this verse highlights the importance of humility in our responses to others. Often, our anger is fueled by pride—by the belief that we have been wronged and that we deserve to be treated better. But Proverbs 19:11 invites us to take a different perspective, one that prioritizes humility and understanding over our own sense of justice. By choosing to pass over a transgression, we acknowledge that we are all imperfect, that we all make mistakes, and that sometimes, it is better to let go of our pride in favor of maintaining harmony and peace. This humility is a crucial aspect of living a life that reflects the character of Christ, who, even when wronged, chose to forgive and show mercy rather than demand retribution.

Moreover, the discretion to defer anger and to pass over a transgression is closely tied to the concept of forgiveness, which is a central theme in the Bible. Forgiveness is not always easy; it often requires us to let go of our desire for justice or retribution and to extend grace to those who have hurt us. However, Proverbs 19:11 suggests that this act of mercy is where true glory lies—not in winning arguments, proving others wrong, or exacting revenge, but in showing the kind of grace that God shows us every day. When we forgive, we are participating in the divine nature of God, who is described as "merciful and gracious, slow to anger, and plenteous in mercy" (Psalm 103:8). This participation in God's mercy allows us to grow spiritually, as we learn to let go of anger and embrace a more peaceful and forgiving way of life.

The verse also encourages us to think about the long-term impact of our actions. While reacting in anger might provide temporary satisfaction, it often leads to lasting negative consequences, such as broken relationships, regret, and a loss of respect from others. In contrast, choosing to defer anger and to forgive can lead to lasting positive outcomes, including stronger relationships, a sense of inner peace, and the respect and admiration of those around us. This long-term perspective is a hallmark of wisdom, as it prioritizes lasting peace and harmony over short-term emotional reactions. It also reflects the understanding that our actions have a ripple effect, influencing not just our own lives but the lives of those around us. By choosing mercy, we create an environment where others feel safe, valued, and respected, which in turn fosters a culture of forgiveness and understanding.

Furthermore, the discretion to defer anger and pass over a transgression is a form of emotional intelligence, which involves being aware of our own emotions, understanding how they affect our behavior, and managing them in a way that is constructive and positive. Emotional intelligence is crucial for navigating the complexities of life, as it allows us to respond to challenges with grace and wisdom rather than being controlled by our emotions. Proverbs 19:11 teaches us that one of the most important aspects of emotional intelligence is the ability to manage our anger and to choose a merciful response, even when we feel justified in our anger. This ability to control our emotions and to respond with grace is what sets wise and mature individuals apart, as it shows a deep understanding of the power of mercy and forgiveness in maintaining healthy relationships and a peaceful life.

Additionally, this verse speaks to the importance of personal responsibility in managing our emotions. While it is natural to feel anger when we are wronged, Proverbs 19:11 reminds us that we have a choice in how we respond to that anger. We can choose to react impulsively, allowing our anger to dictate our actions, or we can choose to defer our anger, taking the time to reflect and respond in a way that is aligned with our values and with God's teachings. This personal responsibility is empowering, as it gives us control over our emotions and our actions, rather than being controlled by them. It also encourages us to take ownership of our behavior and to strive for a life that is characterized by wisdom, mercy, and peace.

Moreover, this verse highlights the role of discretion in maintaining social harmony. In any community or group, conflicts and misunderstandings are bound to arise. However, how we choose to handle these situations can either contribute to peace or to further discord. By exercising discretion and choosing to overlook minor offenses, we can help to maintain a sense of unity and harmony within our communities. This approach fosters a culture of forgiveness and understanding, where people are more likely to give each other the benefit of the doubt and to work towards reconciliation rather than holding onto grudges. This culture of mercy is essential for building strong, supportive, and resilient communities that can withstand the challenges of life together.

In conclusion, Proverbs 19:11 offers profound wisdom on the importance of discretion, mercy, and forgiveness in managing anger and maintaining peace in our lives. The verse encourages us to be mindful of our emotions, to defer our anger, and to choose a merciful response, even when we feel justified in our anger. By doing so, we not only protect our own peace of mind and well-being but also contribute to the harmony and strength of our relationships and communities. The glory that comes from passing over a transgression is not just about avoiding conflict; it is about embodying the principles of love, grace, and forgiveness that are central to the Christian faith. It is about choosing to reflect the character of God in our interactions with others, showing mercy even when it is difficult, and prioritizing peace and reconciliation over pride and retribution. This approach to life requires strength, humility, and wisdom, but the rewards are profound—a life of peace, strong and healthy relationships, and a deeper connection with God. As we strive to live out the teachings of Proverbs 19:11, we are not only living in accordance with God's will but also setting an example for others, showing them the power of mercy and forgiveness in creating a more just, peaceful, and loving world. The discretion to defer anger and to pass over a transgression is a choice that we must make every day, in every interaction, and it is a choice that has the potential to transform our lives and the lives of those around us. Through this merciful approach, we can experience the true glory that comes from living a life that is pleasing to God and that reflects His love and grace in all that we do.

Chapter 7 - The Mellow

Psalm 37:8, "Cease from anger, and forsake wrath: fret not thyself in any wise to do evil," offers a powerful and timeless message about the importance of adopting a mellow attitude, one that encourages us to let go of anger and avoid the destructive paths that anger can lead us down. This verse is a call to rise above the emotions that often lead us into conflict and sin, urging us to embrace a more peaceful and composed approach to life. Anger is a natural human emotion, something that everyone experiences at some point, but the wisdom in this Psalm reminds us that how we handle that anger can define our character and our life's direction. When we allow anger to control us, it can lead to wrath, which is a more intense, long-lasting form of anger that often drives us to act in ways that we later regret. Wrath can fuel thoughts of revenge, create a toxic atmosphere in relationships, and lead us down a path that is far from the peace and righteousness that God desires for us. Psalm 37:8 advises us to "cease from anger," which means to stop, to put an end to the anger that is building up inside us before it has a chance to take root and grow into something more harmful. This is a deliberate choice, a decision to not let anger take hold of our hearts and minds, but instead to release it and seek a calmer, more balanced perspective.

To "forsake wrath" goes even further, urging us to completely abandon the kind of deep-seated anger that festers and can lead to serious harm. Forsaking wrath is about choosing to not let anger dictate our actions or thoughts, to walk away from the temptation to nurse grievances, and to avoid letting anger turn into something more dangerous like bitterness or hatred. Wrath often blinds us to the bigger picture, narrowing our focus to the immediate hurt or offense we feel, and pushing us toward actions that may feel satisfying in the moment but ultimately lead to more pain and suffering for ourselves and others. By advising us to forsake wrath, Psalm 37:8 is guiding us towards a life that is free from the burden of carrying anger and resentment, and instead embracing a way of living that is marked by peace, forgiveness, and emotional freedom. This is not about denying our feelings or pretending that we don't get hurt or angry; it's about learning to process those emotions in a healthy way, without letting them take over our lives.

The verse also cautions against "fretting," which is another way of saying that we should not worry or obsess over the wrongs done to us. Fretting can cause us to dwell on negative thoughts, replaying the offense over and over in our minds, which only serves to keep the anger alive and growing. When we fret, we allow the initial spark of anger to ignite a fire of ongoing resentment, which can consume our thoughts and distract us from the more positive and meaningful aspects of life. This kind of constant worry and rumination can lead to a cycle of negativity, where we are continually focused on what has gone wrong, rather than finding ways to move forward and let go. Psalm 37:8 advises us not to let ourselves get caught up in this cycle, because it can easily lead us down a path where anger controls us rather than us controlling our anger. This warning is crucial because it highlights the connection between our thoughts and our actions—what we dwell on in our minds often translates into how we behave. If we are constantly fretting and worrying about the wrongs done to us, we are more likely to act out of that anger and frustration, leading us to do things we might later regret.

The phrase "in any wise to do evil" is a clear reminder that allowing anger and wrath to dictate our actions can lead us to commit wrongs ourselves. Even if we feel justified in our anger, acting out of that emotion can lead us to make decisions that are harmful, both to ourselves and to others. Anger, when left unchecked, can push us to cross lines we wouldn't normally cross, to say things we wouldn't normally say, and to do things we wouldn't normally do. The verse is a call to self-awareness and self-control, urging us to recognize when our anger is leading us toward destructive behavior and to stop ourselves before we go too far. It's about understanding that while anger itself is not inherently sinful, the actions it can lead to often are. The Bible teaches us that vengeance belongs to God, and when we take matters into our own hands, driven by anger and the desire for retribution, we step outside of God's will for our lives. Instead of giving in to anger and wrath, we are encouraged to trust in God's justice and timing, believing that He will make things right in His own way and in His own time.

Psalm 37:8, therefore, is not just a command to stop being angry, but a deeper invitation to a lifestyle of trust, peace, and reliance on God. It challenges us to let go of the need to control every situation, especially those that make us angry, and to release that control to God. This kind of trust requires faith, believing that God sees the injustices we face and will handle them according to His perfect wisdom. It also requires humility, recognizing that our perspective is limited and that we don't always know the best way to handle every situation, especially when our emotions are high. By ceasing from anger and forsaking wrath, we are not just avoiding sin; we are also embracing a life that is more aligned with God's character—a life that values peace, forgiveness, and righteousness over the temporary satisfaction of acting on our anger.

Moreover, adopting a mellow attitude as urged by Psalm 37:8 has profound implications for our relationships and overall well-being. Anger, especially when it turns into wrath, can be incredibly destructive to our relationships with others. It can create distance, foster mistrust, and build walls where there should be understanding and compassion. By choosing to let go of anger, we open the door to healing and reconciliation. We create space for conversations that can lead to resolution and mutual respect, rather than further conflict. A mellow attitude doesn't mean we ignore issues or allow ourselves to be mistreated; rather, it means we approach situations with a calm and composed mindset, seeking solutions that are constructive rather than destructive. This approach not only strengthens our relationships but also contributes to our own mental and emotional health. Carrying anger and wrath can be a heavy burden, leading to stress, anxiety, and even physical health problems. By letting go of these negative emotions, we free ourselves from that burden, allowing ourselves to experience more peace, joy, and contentment in life.

In addition, Psalm 37:8 encourages us to think about the broader impact of our actions. When we choose to cease from anger and forsake wrath, we are not just making a personal decision; we are also influencing the atmosphere around us. Our attitudes and behaviors have a ripple effect, impacting the people we interact with and the environments we are part of. A person who consistently responds to challenges with a mellow attitude can be a calming and stabilizing presence, helping to diffuse tension and create a more positive and peaceful atmosphere. On the other hand, a person who is quick to anger and prone to wrath can contribute to a culture of conflict and hostility, where misunderstandings and disputes are more likely to escalate. By embracing the teachings of Psalm 37:8, we become agents of peace, contributing to a more harmonious and compassionate world.

Furthermore, this verse encourages us to reflect on the long-term consequences of our actions. Anger and wrath may provide a temporary sense of relief or satisfaction, but they often lead to long-term negative consequences, both for ourselves and for others. Relationships can be damaged, opportunities can be lost, and our own sense of inner peace can be compromised. By choosing to let go of anger and embrace a more mellow attitude, we are investing in a future that is more peaceful, stable, and fulfilling. This long-term perspective is a key aspect of wisdom, as it encourages us to look beyond the immediate moment and consider the bigger picture. It's about recognizing that our actions today have consequences that can last far into the future, and choosing to act in ways that lead to positive outcomes, both for ourselves and for those around us.

In conclusion, Psalm 37:8 offers a powerful and practical guide for managing anger and living a life that is marked by peace, wisdom, and trust in God. By advising us to cease from anger, forsake wrath, and not fret ourselves in any wise to do evil, this verse calls us to adopt a mellow attitude that prioritizes forgiveness, understanding, and self-control. It encourages us to let go of the negative emotions that can lead us down destructive paths and to instead embrace a way of living that is more aligned with God's character and desires for us. This approach not only protects our relationships and well-being but also allows us to contribute to a more peaceful and compassionate world. By following the teachings of Psalm 37:8, we can free ourselves from the burden of anger and experience the peace and joy that come from living a life that is rooted in trust, humility, and love. This verse is a timeless reminder of the power of choosing peace over conflict, and the profound impact that choice can have on our lives and the lives of those around us.

Chapter 8 – The Mature

Colossians 3:8, "But now ye also put off all these; anger, wrath, malice, blasphemy, filthy communication out of your mouth," is a verse that calls for a mature rejection of destructive behaviors and emotions, emphasizing the importance of spiritual growth and self-discipline in the life of a believer. This passage is a direct appeal to cast aside the negative traits and tendencies that hinder our ability to live in accordance with the teachings of Christ. At its core, this verse highlights the need for personal transformation and the pursuit of a higher standard of living—one that reflects the values of the Christian faith and the character of Christ. Anger and wrath are among the first things mentioned, and they are emotions that, while natural, can become deeply destructive if not properly managed. Anger can often be justified by our circumstances, but Colossians 3:8 challenges us to not simply justify our anger but to put it off entirely. This does not mean ignoring or suppressing our feelings, but rather, it involves recognizing when anger begins to take control and deciding to respond in a way that reflects maturity and self-control. Wrath, which is an intensified and prolonged form of anger, is similarly called out as something that needs to be put off—forsaken because it can lead to harmful actions and words that damage relationships and our own spiritual well-being.

The verse continues by urging us to put off malice, which is an intention or desire to do evil or harm to others. Malice goes beyond momentary anger or frustration; it is a settled state of ill will that corrodes the heart and mind, leading to actions that are meant to hurt or destroy. When we hold onto malice, we are allowing negative emotions to dictate our actions, which is the opposite of the maturity and self-discipline that Colossians 3:8 is advocating for. To be mature in our faith means to reject malice in all its forms, to refuse to let bitterness or hatred take root in our hearts. This requires a conscious effort to forgive those who have wronged us, to seek reconciliation where possible, and to move forward with a spirit of grace and understanding. Maturity is demonstrated not just in what we refrain from doing, but in the positive actions we choose to take instead—actions that build others up, rather than tear them down.

Blasphemy is another behavior that believers are urged to put off. In this context, blasphemy refers to speaking with disrespect about God or sacred things, but it can also extend to any form of disrespectful or hurtful speech directed towards others. Words have immense power; they can uplift and encourage, or they can wound and destroy. Blasphemy and other forms of harmful speech are often fueled by anger, frustration, or malice, and they reflect a lack of maturity and self-control. Colossians 3:8 calls us to a higher standard of communication, one that reflects the love and respect we are called to show both to God and to our fellow human beings. To put off blasphemy means to choose words that are thoughtful, kind, and constructive, even in moments of anger or disagreement. It is a call to rise above the temptation to lash out verbally and instead speak in ways that reflect the character of Christ.

The final behavior mentioned in Colossians 3:8 is "filthy communication out of your mouth," which encompasses all forms of inappropriate or harmful speech, including lying, gossiping, slandering, and using foul language. Filthy communication not only reflects poorly on the individual but also creates a toxic environment that can harm relationships and communities. This kind of speech often stems from unchecked emotions like anger, frustration, or resentment, and it can quickly spiral out of control, causing significant damage. The maturity that Colossians 3:8 calls for involves being mindful of the words we speak, understanding that what comes out of our mouths is a reflection of what is in our hearts. To put off filthy communication is to commit to speaking with integrity, honesty, and kindness, and to reject the urge to use words as weapons. It is about creating an environment where others feel safe, valued, and respected, and where conversations are uplifting and edifying rather than destructive.

The overall message of Colossians 3:8 is one of transformation and renewal. The phrase "put off" suggests that these behaviors and emotions are like old clothes that no longer fit who we are becoming in Christ. As believers, we are called to shed these old ways and to embrace a new way of living—one that is characterized by love, peace, and righteousness. This process of putting off the old and putting on the new is central to the Christian journey, and it requires ongoing effort and commitment. It is a call to maturity, to grow beyond the behaviors and attitudes that once defined us, and to become more like Christ in our thoughts, words, and actions. Maturity in this context is not about age or experience, but about the willingness to let go of what is harmful and embrace what is good and true.

Moreover, this verse speaks to the importance of self-awareness and self-discipline in the process of spiritual growth. To put off anger, wrath, malice, blasphemy, and filthy communication requires us to first recognize these behaviors in ourselves, to be honest about the areas where we struggle, and to seek God's help in overcoming them. It is a process that involves both personal effort and divine assistance, as we rely on the Holy Spirit to guide and empower us in our journey toward maturity. This self-awareness is a crucial aspect of maturity, as it allows us to see ourselves clearly, to acknowledge our shortcomings, and to take steps toward positive change. It also requires humility, as we must be willing to admit that we are not yet who we are called to be and that we need God's grace to help us grow.

The call to maturity in Colossians 3:8 is also a call to live in community with others in a way that reflects the values of the Kingdom of God. The behaviors that we are urged to put off—anger, wrath, malice, blasphemy, and filthy communication—are all things that can harm relationships and disrupt the unity of the body of Christ. By rejecting these behaviors, we are choosing to build up rather than tear down, to promote peace rather than discord, and to create an environment where love and respect can flourish. This is not just about personal growth, but about contributing to the health and well-being of the community as a whole. Maturity in this context involves taking responsibility for the impact of our actions on others and striving to live in a way that brings glory to God and benefits those around us.

In addition, Colossians 3:8 challenges us to consider the deeper motivations behind our actions and words. Anger, wrath, malice, blasphemy, and filthy communication often arise from unresolved issues within our hearts, such as insecurity, fear, or a desire for control. To truly put off these behaviors, we must address the root causes and seek healing and transformation at a deeper level. This may involve examining our own attitudes and beliefs, seeking forgiveness for past wrongs, and allowing God to work in our hearts to bring about lasting change. Maturity, therefore, is not just about changing our outward behavior, but about allowing God to renew us from the inside out, so that our actions and words naturally reflect the character of Christ.

Furthermore, the verse implies that this process of putting off the old and embracing the new is not a one-time event, but an ongoing journey. As we grow in our faith, we will continually be challenged to let go of old habits and attitudes that no longer serve us and to embrace new ways of thinking and behaving that are more in line with our identity in Christ. This process requires patience and perseverance, as well as a willingness to continually seek God's guidance and strength. Maturity involves recognizing that we are all works in progress, and that true growth takes time and effort. It also involves extending grace to ourselves and others as we navigate this journey, understanding that we will all have setbacks and struggles along the way.

In conclusion, Colossians 3:8 is a powerful call to maturity in the Christian life, urging us to reject the behaviors and attitudes that hinder our spiritual growth and to embrace a new way of living that reflects the character of Christ. By putting off anger, wrath, malice, blasphemy, and filthy communication, we are choosing to live in a way that promotes peace, love, and unity within the body of Christ. This process of transformation requires self-awareness, self-discipline, and a deep reliance on God's grace, as we seek to grow in our faith and become more like Christ in our thoughts, words, and actions. The maturity that Colossians 3:8 calls for is not about perfection, but about a commitment to continual growth and a willingness to let go of what is harmful and embrace what is good and true. It is about living in a way that reflects the values of the Kingdom of God and contributes to the well-being of the community as a whole. As we strive to live out this call to maturity, we can trust that God is with us every step of the way, guiding us, strengthening us, and helping us to become the people He has called us to be.

Chapter 9 – The Mediation

Proverbs 15:18, "A wrathful man stirreth up strife: but he that is slow to anger appeaseth strife," provides a powerful and practical lesson on the importance of controlling our anger to promote peace and understanding, emphasizing the role of mediation in maintaining harmony in our relationships and communities. Anger, while a natural and sometimes unavoidable emotion, can easily spiral out of control if not managed properly, leading to conflict, hurt, and division. This verse draws a clear contrast between two types of people: the wrathful person, who allows anger to dominate their actions and reactions, and the person who is slow to anger, who exercises patience and restraint, becoming a peacemaker rather than a source of conflict. The wrathful person, driven by intense, unchecked emotions, tends to stir up strife wherever they go. Strife, in this context, refers to bitter disagreement, discord, and conflict—an environment where peace is shattered, and relationships are strained. When anger is allowed to take the lead, it often results in harsh words, impulsive decisions, and actions that are regretted later. This kind of behavior can create a cycle of negativity, where one angry outburst leads to another, escalating the situation and causing more harm than good. The wrathful man, as described in Proverbs 15:18, becomes a catalyst for ongoing conflict, unable to see beyond his immediate emotions and the desire to express his anger, regardless of the consequences.

In contrast, the person who is slow to anger, who takes time to cool down before responding, has the ability to "appease strife." To appease means to calm, pacify, or bring to a state of peace. This individual understands the value of mediation—the process of intervening in a dispute to resolve it peacefully. By being slow to anger, they create space for thoughtful reflection, allowing themselves to consider the situation from multiple angles and to understand the perspectives of others involved. This approach often leads to better outcomes because it fosters an environment where communication and understanding can thrive, rather than one dominated by hostility and resentment. Mediation, in this sense, is not just about resolving conflicts after they have arisen, but about preventing them from escalating in the first place. The person who is slow to anger recognizes that anger, while sometimes justified, must be tempered with wisdom and patience to avoid unnecessary strife.

The concept of being "slow to anger" in Proverbs 15:18 is closely linked to the idea of emotional intelligence—the ability to recognize, understand, and manage our own emotions, as well as to recognize and influence the emotions of others. Emotional intelligence plays a crucial role in mediation, as it allows individuals to approach conflicts with empathy and a clear mind, rather than reacting impulsively out of anger. By taking a step back and giving themselves time to think, those who are slow to anger are better equipped to handle difficult situations with grace and composure. This does not mean suppressing or ignoring anger, but rather, it involves acknowledging the emotion, understanding its source, and choosing a response that aligns with long-term goals of peace and reconciliation, rather than short-term emotional release. This approach not only helps to de-escalate tensions but also sets a positive example for others, showing that it is possible to address issues calmly and constructively.

Furthermore, Proverbs 15:18 highlights the role of patience in maintaining peace. Patience is often described as a virtue, and in the context of anger and conflict, it is a critical component of successful mediation. Being slow to anger requires patience—patience with ourselves, as we work through our emotions, and patience with others, as we seek to understand their perspectives and find common ground. This patience allows us to avoid reacting in the heat of the moment, when our judgment is most likely to be clouded by anger. Instead, it gives us the time and space needed to respond in a way that is thoughtful, measured, and likely to lead to a positive outcome. Patience also helps to build trust, as it shows others that we are willing to listen, to consider their views, and to work together towards a peaceful resolution. This trust is essential in any mediation process, as it encourages open communication and collaboration, making it easier to reach a mutually acceptable solution.

In addition to patience, humility is another key quality that underpins the ability to be slow to anger and to mediate conflicts effectively. Humility involves recognizing that we do not have all the answers and that our perspective is not the only valid one. It requires us to set aside our pride and the desire to always be right, in order to truly listen to others and to consider their feelings and viewpoints. In the context of Proverbs 15:18, humility helps to temper our anger, as it reminds us that our anger, while real and valid, should not override the importance of maintaining peace and harmony in our relationships. A humble approach to conflict recognizes that everyone involved has their own experiences, emotions, and reasons for feeling the way they do, and that these need to be respected and addressed in a fair and balanced way. By embracing humility, we become better mediators, more capable of resolving conflicts in a way that honors all parties involved and leads to lasting peace.

Moreover, the verse suggests that the ability to appease strife through being slow to anger is not only beneficial for the immediate situation but also has broader implications for the overall well-being of a community. When conflicts are managed well, with anger being kept in check and mediation being prioritized, the entire community benefits. Peaceful resolution of conflicts strengthens relationships, fosters a sense of mutual respect, and creates an environment where individuals feel safe and supported. This, in turn, contributes to the overall health and stability of the community, making it a place where people can thrive and work together effectively. On the other hand, when anger and wrath are allowed to dominate, strife can spread, creating divisions, weakening bonds, and leading to an atmosphere of distrust and hostility. Proverbs 15:18, therefore, highlights the importance of individual responsibility in maintaining the peace and well-being of the broader community. By being slow to anger and focusing on mediation, we each contribute to creating a more harmonious and supportive environment for everyone.

In conclusion, Proverbs 15:18 offers timeless wisdom on the importance of controlling anger and promoting mediation as a means of maintaining peace and resolving conflicts. The verse clearly contrasts the destructive nature of unchecked anger, which stirs up strife, with the constructive power of being slow to anger, which can appease and prevent strife. By encouraging us to be slow to anger, the verse calls for a mature, thoughtful approach to conflict resolution, one that prioritizes patience, humility, and emotional intelligence. It reminds us that while anger is a natural emotion, it must be managed carefully to avoid causing harm to ourselves and others. Through mediation, we can turn potential conflicts into opportunities for growth, understanding, and strengthened relationships. This approach not only benefits us individually but also contributes to the overall health and harmony of our communities, making Proverbs 15:18 a vital guide for anyone seeking to live a life marked by peace, wisdom, and compassion.

Chapter 10 – The Measured

Ecclesiastes 7:9, "Be not hasty in thy spirit to be angry: for anger resteth in the bosom of fools," is a verse that offers profound wisdom on the dangers of quick anger and the importance of adopting a measured, thoughtful approach to our emotions. This verse speaks to the very essence of emotional intelligence, urging us to slow down and consider our reactions before allowing anger to take hold. Anger is a powerful emotion, one that can arise suddenly and with great intensity, often catching us off guard and compelling us to react in ways that we might later regret. The wisdom of Ecclesiastes 7:9 lies in its warning against the impulsiveness of quick anger, which the verse equates with foolishness. When we are hasty to anger, we are essentially giving in to our most basic, instinctual reactions without taking the time to think through the consequences of our actions or to understand the full context of the situation. This hastiness can lead to decisions and behaviors that are not only unwise but also harmful, both to ourselves and to those around us.

The phrase "anger resteth in the bosom of fools" vividly illustrates the folly of allowing anger to dwell within us. To "rest" in this context suggests a kind of settled, enduring presence, implying that once anger takes root, it can be difficult to dislodge. Anger that is allowed to linger in our hearts can lead to bitterness, resentment, and a host of other negative emotions that cloud our judgment and distort our perceptions. The verse implies that those who are quick to anger, who let it settle in their hearts without questioning or managing it, are acting foolishly because they are letting an emotion control them rather than exercising control over the emotion. This is why the verse advises a measured approach to anger—one that involves pausing, reflecting, and carefully considering our response before we act. Such an approach requires self-discipline and a willingness to resist the immediate gratification that often comes from expressing our anger in the heat of the moment.

The call to "be not hasty in thy spirit to be angry" is a reminder that our initial reactions to situations are not always the best or the wisest. When we encounter something that provokes us, whether it be a slight, an insult, or an injustice, our natural inclination might be to react with anger, to defend ourselves, or to strike back. However, Ecclesiastes 7:9 encourages us to take a step back and allow ourselves the time to process our emotions before responding. This measured approach is not about suppressing or denying our feelings; rather, it is about giving ourselves the space to ensure that our response is appropriate, constructive, and in line with our values and long-term goals. By doing so, we can avoid the pitfalls of quick anger, such as saying or doing things that we might later regret, damaging relationships, or escalating conflicts unnecessarily.

Moreover, the verse suggests that quick anger is a sign of immaturity and a lack of wisdom. In contrast, those who are able to manage their anger and approach situations with calm and deliberation demonstrate maturity and emotional intelligence. This maturity involves recognizing that anger, while a valid and sometimes necessary emotion, should not be the driving force behind our decisions or actions. It is about understanding that while we cannot always control the situations that provoke us, we can control how we choose to respond. By taking a measured approach to anger, we can navigate challenging situations with greater wisdom, clarity, and effectiveness, ultimately leading to better outcomes for ourselves and those around us.

The wisdom of Ecclesiastes 7:9 is especially relevant in today's fast-paced world, where we are often encouraged to react quickly and decisively, sometimes at the expense of careful consideration and reflection. Whether in our personal lives, in our relationships, or in our work, the pressure to respond immediately can lead us to make hasty decisions that are not always in our best interest. This verse challenges us to slow down, to resist the urge to react impulsively, and to take the time to ensure that our actions are thoughtful and measured. By doing so, we can avoid the negative consequences that often accompany quick anger, such as damaged relationships, lost opportunities, and unnecessary conflict.

In addition, the verse highlights the importance of patience and long-suffering as virtues that counteract the tendency toward quick anger. Patience allows us to endure provocation without immediately reacting in anger, giving us the time to consider the situation from different perspectives and to respond in a way that is more aligned with our values and long-term goals. Long-suffering, which is the ability to endure hardship or suffering with patience, further reinforces the idea that we should not be quick to anger, even in difficult or trying circumstances. These virtues are essential for maintaining peace in our relationships and for ensuring that we do not allow anger to take root in our hearts and lead us down a path of folly.

Furthermore, the verse implies that quick anger is often a reflection of underlying issues within ourselves—issues such as insecurity, pride, or a lack of self-control. When we are quick to anger, it may be because we feel threatened, disrespected, or powerless, and we use anger as a way to assert ourselves or to regain a sense of control. However, Ecclesiastes 7:9 challenges us to look beyond these surface-level reactions and to address the deeper issues that may be driving our anger. By doing so, we can develop a greater sense of self-awareness and emotional intelligence, which in turn enables us to respond to situations with greater wisdom and maturity.

The verse also encourages us to consider the impact of our anger on others. When we are quick to anger, we are not only putting ourselves at risk of making foolish decisions, but we are also creating a negative environment for those around us. Anger can be contagious, spreading quickly and causing others to react in kind, leading to a cycle of conflict and strife. By taking a measured approach to anger, we can break this cycle and create an environment that is more conducive to peace, understanding, and mutual respect. This is especially important in our relationships, where quick anger can lead to misunderstandings, hurt feelings, and long-lasting damage. By choosing to be slow to anger, we can foster healthier, more positive relationships that are built on a foundation of trust and communication.

In conclusion, Ecclesiastes 7:9 offers timeless wisdom on the dangers of quick anger and the importance of adopting a measured, thoughtful approach to our emotions. The verse calls us to resist the impulse to react hastily in anger, recognizing that such impulsiveness is a sign of folly and can lead to negative consequences for ourselves and others. Instead, we are encouraged to take a step back, to reflect, and to ensure that our response is calm, considered, and in line with our values and long-term goals. By doing so, we can avoid the pitfalls of quick anger, such as damaging relationships, escalating conflicts, and making decisions that we later regret. This measured approach to anger is a sign of maturity and emotional intelligence, qualities that are essential for living a life of wisdom, peace, and fulfillment. In a world that often values quick reactions and decisive action, Ecclesiastes 7:9 reminds us of the importance of patience, self-control, and thoughtful reflection in managing our emotions and making wise decisions. By embracing the wisdom of this verse, we can navigate the challenges of life with greater clarity and effectiveness, ultimately leading to better outcomes for ourselves and those around us.

Chapter 11 – The Mercy

Romans 12:19, "Dearly beloved, avenge not yourselves, but rather give place unto wrath: for it is written, Vengeance is mine; I will repay, saith the Lord," offers profound wisdom about the power of mercy and the importance of entrusting justice to God rather than taking matters into our own hands. This verse serves as a powerful reminder that in moments of anger, when we feel wronged or hurt by others, the natural inclination might be to seek revenge or to make those who have hurt us suffer in return. However, Romans 12:19 encourages us to resist this impulse and to instead choose a path of mercy and trust in God's justice. The idea of "avenging not yourselves" goes against the grain of human nature, where the instinct for retaliation is strong, especially when we feel deeply wronged. It challenges us to rise above these instincts and to embrace a higher calling—a calling that reflects the love, patience, and mercy that God extends to us. The command to "give place unto wrath" means that we are to step aside, allowing room for God's judgment rather than letting our own anger dictate our actions. It is an invitation to let go of the need to control the outcome of a situation and to trust that God, who is just and all-knowing, will handle it in His perfect way and timing.

The concept of leaving vengeance to God is deeply rooted in the understanding that human judgment is often clouded by emotion, particularly by anger and the desire for revenge. When we are hurt or offended, our perspective can become narrow, focused only on our pain and the perceived injustice we have suffered. In this state, it is easy to lose sight of the broader picture, to overlook the complexities of the situation, and to react in ways that may cause more harm than good. Romans 12:19 reminds us that our ability to judge and to administer justice is limited and that in our anger, we are prone to act unwisely or even unjustly. By choosing to leave vengeance to God, we acknowledge our limitations and entrust the situation to the One who sees all, knows all, and judges with perfect righteousness. This act of surrender is not a sign of weakness but of strength and wisdom, recognizing that true justice belongs to God and that His ways are higher than ours.

Moreover, the verse speaks to the transformative power of mercy. When we choose not to avenge ourselves, we are making a conscious decision to break the cycle of anger and retaliation that so often leads to escalating conflict and further harm. Mercy, in this context, is about more than just withholding punishment; it is about choosing a different path—a path that leads to healing, reconciliation, and peace. By showing mercy, we open the door to possibilities that vengeance would close off. We allow for the potential of restoration, for relationships to be mended, and for hearts to be softened. Mercy transforms not only the person who receives it but also the person who gives it. It frees us from the burden of carrying anger and resentment, allowing us to move forward with a sense of peace and freedom that vengeance could never provide. In this way, mercy is a gift that we give to ourselves as much as to others.

Romans 12:19 also teaches us about the importance of trusting in God's justice. The phrase "Vengeance is mine; I will repay, saith the Lord" is a powerful declaration of God's sovereignty and justice. It reassures us that no wrong goes unnoticed by God, and that He will ensure that justice is served in His time and in His way. This trust in God's justice allows us to release our anger and our desire for revenge, knowing that we do not need to take matters into our own hands. It is a call to faith, to believe that God is in control and that He will make things right, even when we cannot see how or when. This trust is a form of worship, an acknowledgment that God is sovereign and that His ways are perfect, even when they are beyond our understanding. By leaving vengeance to God, we are placing our faith in His goodness and His perfect justice, and we are allowing ourselves to rest in the peace that comes from knowing that He is in control.

Furthermore, the verse encourages us to reflect on the example of Jesus, who embodied this teaching in His own life and ministry. Jesus, who was wronged in the most profound ways, chose not to seek vengeance but to forgive and to show mercy, even to those who persecuted and crucified Him. His life is the ultimate example of what it means to "avenge not yourselves" and to trust in God's justice. Jesus' response to those who wronged Him was not one of anger or retaliation, but of love, forgiveness, and a deep trust in His Father's will. This example challenges us to consider how we, too, can respond with mercy and grace when we are wronged, and how we can entrust our pain and our need for justice to God.

The verse also has practical implications for how we live our daily lives and interact with others. In a world that often values retribution and sees mercy as a weakness, Romans 12:19 calls us to live counter-culturally, to reject the norms of vengeance and to embrace the radical call to mercy. This can be challenging, especially in situations where we feel deeply wronged or where justice seems delayed or denied. However, the verse reminds us that by choosing mercy, we are not condoning wrongdoing, but rather, we are placing our trust in a higher justice—God's justice. This choice to show mercy can have a profound impact on our relationships, our communities, and our world. It can bring about peace where there was conflict, healing where there was hurt, and reconciliation where there was division.

In addition, the verse encourages us to consider the long-term consequences of our actions. When we choose to take vengeance into our own hands, we often set in motion a cycle of retaliation that can lead to escalating conflict and further harm. This cycle can be difficult to break and can cause lasting damage to relationships and communities. In contrast, when we choose to leave vengeance to God and to show mercy, we are contributing to a cycle of peace and reconciliation. We are planting seeds of forgiveness and grace that can bear fruit in ways we may never fully see or understand. This long-term perspective is a key aspect of wisdom, as it encourages us to look beyond our immediate feelings of hurt and anger and to consider the bigger picture—one that includes the possibility of healing, restoration, and the building of a more just and compassionate world.

Moreover, Romans 12:19 invites us to reflect on the role of humility in our lives. Choosing not to avenge ourselves requires humility—a recognition that we do not have all the answers, that we are not in control, and that we are not the ultimate judges of right and wrong. Humility allows us to step back, to let go of our pride, and to trust in God's wisdom and justice. It also enables us to see others with compassion, to recognize that they, too, are flawed and in need of mercy, just as we are. This humility is essential for living a life of mercy and for building relationships that are grounded in love, respect, and mutual understanding.

The verse also speaks to the freedom that comes from choosing mercy over vengeance. When we hold onto anger and seek revenge, we are often held captive by our own emotions, unable to move forward and to find peace. Vengeance can consume us, leaving us trapped in a cycle of bitterness and resentment. In contrast, when we choose to leave vengeance to God and to show mercy, we free ourselves from this cycle. We release the burden of anger and allow ourselves to experience the peace and joy that come from trusting in God's justice. This freedom is a gift, one that allows us to live more fully and to focus on the things that truly matter—our relationships, our faith, and our growth as individuals.

In conclusion, Romans 12:19 offers a powerful and transformative message about the importance of mercy and the wisdom of leaving vengeance to God. The verse challenges us to resist the natural impulse to seek revenge and to instead place our trust in God's perfect justice. By choosing mercy, we break the cycle of anger and retaliation, paving the way for peace, healing, and reconciliation. This act of mercy not only benefits those who receive it but also frees us from the burden of anger and allows us to live more fully and joyfully. The verse also encourages us to reflect on the example of Jesus, who embodied this teaching in His own life and who calls us to follow in His footsteps. By embracing the wisdom of Romans 12:19, we can build a life that is grounded in love, humility, and trust in God, and that contributes to the creation of a more just and compassionate world. This call to mercy is not an easy one, but it is a path that leads to true peace and fulfillment, both for ourselves and for those around us.

Chapter 12 – The Mindful

Proverbs 22:24-25, "Make no friendship with an angry man; and with a furious man thou shalt not go: Lest thou learn his ways, and get a snare to thy soul," offers timeless wisdom on the importance of being mindful about the company we keep, especially in relation to anger and its influence on our behavior and character. This verse underscores the powerful impact that our relationships and associations can have on our own actions, attitudes, and ultimately, our soul. It advises caution in forming close bonds with those who are quick to anger or are characterized by fury, not because we are to judge or dismiss others, but because of the very real risk that their negative traits can rub off on us, leading us down a path of negativity and potential destruction. The verse uses the metaphor of a "snare to thy soul," which vividly illustrates how dangerous it can be to absorb the habits and behaviors of those who are driven by anger. A snare is a trap, something that is designed to catch and hold its victim, preventing them from moving forward or escaping. When we surround ourselves with individuals who are constantly angry or furious, their influence can become a snare to our own souls, trapping us in a cycle of negativity, bitterness, and even conflict that can be difficult to break free from.

The wisdom in Proverbs 22:24-25 is deeply rooted in the understanding that humans are inherently social creatures, and we are influenced, often more than we realize, by the attitudes, behaviors, and values of those we spend the most time with. This influence can be positive, leading us to grow, learn, and become better versions of ourselves, or it can be negative, dragging us down and leading us into behaviors and mindsets that are harmful. The verse specifically warns against forming close friendships with those who are angry or furious because these emotions, when unchecked, can lead to a host of other negative behaviors, such as resentment, revenge, and violence. Anger is a powerful emotion, and when it is not managed properly, it can quickly spiral out of control, affecting not only the individual who harbors it but also those around them. By advising us to avoid close relationships with angry individuals, Proverbs 22:24-25 is essentially encouraging us to protect our own hearts and minds from the corrosive effects of anger.

This does not mean that we should abandon or ignore people who struggle with anger, but rather that we should be mindful of the extent to which we allow their anger to influence us. It is important to recognize that while we can and should support others in their personal growth, we must also safeguard our own spiritual and emotional well-being. When anger is a dominant force in someone's life, it can create an environment of constant tension, conflict, and negativity, which can be exhausting and damaging to those who are close to them. Over time, spending too much time in such an environment can cause us to adopt similar attitudes and behaviors, even if we do not initially share them. This is why the verse warns against "learning his ways"—because the more we are exposed to anger and fury, the more likely we are to begin justifying, excusing, or even adopting these emotions as our own. This gradual shift can be subtle, often happening without our conscious awareness, which makes it all the more dangerous.

Furthermore, the verse highlights the importance of choosing our friends and close companions with care. Friendships are one of the most significant influences in our lives, and the people we choose to surround ourselves with can have a profound impact on our character, decisions, and overall direction in life. By advising us to avoid friendships with angry or furious individuals, Proverbs 22:24-25 is encouraging us to seek out relationships that are uplifting, positive, and nurturing—relationships that help us grow in wisdom, patience, and love. These are the kinds of relationships that will support us in becoming the best versions of ourselves, rather than dragging us down into negative patterns of behavior. The verse calls us to be intentional about our relationships, to seek out friends who embody the qualities we aspire to cultivate in ourselves, and to distance ourselves from those who consistently exhibit harmful behaviors.

In addition, the warning in Proverbs 22:24-25 can be understood as a call to be mindful of the broader environments and communities we choose to be a part of. Just as individuals can influence us through their behavior and attitudes, so too can the collective atmosphere of a group, community, or social circle. If we find ourselves in environments where anger, conflict, and negativity are the norm, we are more likely to absorb these traits and begin to see them as acceptable or even inevitable. Conversely, if we seek out environments that are characterized by peace, kindness, and mutual respect, we are more likely to internalize these values and reflect them in our own lives. This is why it is so important to be discerning about the places and groups we choose to associate with, as they can have a significant impact on our spiritual and emotional health.

The phrase "get a snare to thy soul" also suggests the long-term consequences of allowing anger to take root in our lives. Anger, when unchecked, can lead to bitterness, resentment, and a hardened heart—all of which can create a barrier between us and others, as well as between us and God. This is the snare that Proverbs 22:24-25 warns against: the gradual but dangerous shift from occasional anger to a state of being where anger becomes a defining characteristic, shaping our thoughts, actions, and relationships. Once this snare is in place, it can be incredibly difficult to break free from, as it requires not only a change in behavior but also a deep transformation of the heart and mind. This is why it is so important to be vigilant and proactive in guarding against the influence of anger, both in ourselves and in those we choose to associate with.

Moreover, the verse highlights the need for self-awareness and introspection in our relationships. It is not enough to simply avoid angry individuals; we must also be aware of the ways in which our own attitudes and behaviors might contribute to or be influenced by anger. This requires us to take an honest look at our own hearts, to recognize when we are being drawn into patterns of anger or negativity, and to take steps to address these issues before they take root. This might involve seeking out positive influences, practicing forgiveness and patience, or simply taking a step back from situations or relationships that are causing us to feel angry or frustrated. By being mindful in this way, we can protect ourselves from the snare of anger and cultivate a spirit of peace and contentment.

In addition, the verse serves as a reminder of the importance of setting boundaries in our relationships. While it is important to show compassion and support to others, especially those who are struggling with anger or other negative emotions, it is equally important to recognize our own limits and to protect our own well-being. This might mean distancing ourselves from relationships that are consistently harmful or toxic, or simply being more intentional about the time and energy we invest in certain relationships. Setting boundaries is not about rejecting or judging others, but about recognizing the impact that their behavior can have on us and taking steps to protect ourselves from negative influences. By doing so, we are better able to maintain our own peace and well-being, which in turn allows us to be more effective in supporting and helping others.

Furthermore, Proverbs 22:24-25 highlights the importance of being a positive influence in the lives of others. Just as we are warned against the negative impact that angry individuals can have on us, so too are we called to be mindful of the impact that our own behavior has on those around us. This means striving to be a source of peace, kindness, and understanding in our relationships, rather than allowing our own anger or frustration to influence others negatively. It also means being a role model for others, demonstrating through our actions and attitudes the value of patience, forgiveness, and love. By doing so, we can help to create a positive and supportive environment that encourages growth, healing, and mutual respect.

In conclusion, Proverbs 22:24-25 offers timeless wisdom on the importance of being mindful in our relationships and associations, particularly when it comes to anger. The verse warns us of the dangers of forming close bonds with those who are quick to anger or who are characterized by fury, as their negative traits can easily influence us and lead us down a path of negativity and potential destruction. By advising us to avoid these associations, the verse encourages us to seek out relationships that are uplifting, positive, and nurturing—relationships that help us grow in wisdom, patience, and love. It also calls us to be mindful of the environments we choose to be a part of and to set boundaries in our relationships to protect our own well-being. Moreover, the verse serves as a reminder of the importance of being a positive influence in the lives of others, demonstrating through our actions and attitudes the value of patience, forgiveness, and love. By being mindful in these ways, we can protect ourselves from the snare of anger and cultivate a spirit of peace and contentment, ultimately leading to a more fulfilling and harmonious life.

Conclusion

As we come to the end of "Biblical Counsel on Anger", it's important to reflect on the journey we've taken together through Scripture, exploring what God's Word has to say about this powerful emotion. We've seen that anger, while natural and sometimes even justified, is something that needs careful management to prevent it from leading us down a destructive path. Throughout this book, we've discovered that the Bible offers clear guidance on how to deal with anger in ways that honor God and promote peace. From the wisdom of Proverbs, which teaches us to be slow to anger, to the teachings of Jesus, who calls us to forgive and love even when we feel wronged, the Bible provides us with the tools we need to handle anger in a healthy and constructive manner. We've also learned about the dangers of letting anger fester—how it can turn into bitterness, damage our relationships, and pull us away from the peace that God wants us to experience. But most importantly, we've seen that with God's help, we can overcome the negative effects of anger. By turning to prayer, seeking the Holy Spirit's guidance, and applying biblical principles in our daily lives, we can transform our anger into an opportunity for growth, healing, and stronger relationships. This journey through Scripture has shown us that managing anger isn't just about controlling our temper—it's about living in a way that reflects the love, patience, and forgiveness of Christ. As you move forward, I encourage you to keep these lessons close to your heart. Whenever anger arises, remember the wisdom you've gained from God's Word and let it guide your thoughts and actions. Choose to be a peacemaker, someone who brings calm to a situation rather than adding fuel to the fire. Remember that God is always with you, ready to help you navigate your emotions and lead you towards a more peaceful and fulfilling life. The principles you've learned here are not just for today, but for every day of your life. Let them shape how you respond to challenges, how you interact with others, and how you grow in your faith. In doing so, you'll find that you're not just managing anger—you're building a life that honors God and brings peace to those around you. So as you close this book, carry its lessons with you, and trust that God will continue to work in your heart, helping you to live out the biblical counsel on anger that you've learned.

Don't miss out!

Visit the website below and you can sign up to receive emails whenever Joshua Rhoades publishes a new book. There's no charge and no obligation.

https://books2read.com/r/B-A-AJLBB-GSGYE

BOOKS 2 READ

Connecting independent readers to independent writers.

Did you love *Biblical Counsel on Anger*? Then you should read *Renewed Hope- How to Find Encouragement in God*[1] by Joshua Rhoades!

[2]

In a world where challenges and hardships seem to come at us from every side, it's easy to feel overwhelmed, discouraged, and even hopeless. We all face moments when we wonder how we will ever make it through the difficulties we encounter. But in these times, the Bible offers us a powerful example of finding strength and hope, no matter the circumstances. In 1 Samuel 30:6, we read about David, a man who faced great trials and overwhelming odds, yet in the midst of it all, "David encouraged himself in the LORD his God." This simple yet profound statement serves as the foundation for this book, "Renewed Hope- How to Find Encouragement in God." David's life was filled with ups and downs, moments of triumph and times of deep despair. He knew what it was like to be pursued by enemies, to experience loss, and to feel abandoned. Yet, even in his darkest hours, David found a way to renew his hope by turning to God. He didn't rely on his own strength or seek comfort in worldly solutions. Instead, he looked to the LORD, drawing strength and encouragement from his relationship with God. This book is an invitation to explore how we, too, can find renewed hope and

---

1. https://books2read.com/u/boeko1

2. https://books2read.com/u/boeko1

encouragement in God, just as David did. It is a guide to understanding the power of faith, prayer, and trusting in God's promises, even when life seems unbearable. Throughout these pages, we will explore practical ways to draw closer to God, to encourage ourselves in Him, and to discover the peace and strength that come from relying on the LORD. Whether you are facing a specific challenge right now or simply want to deepen your relationship with God, this book will provide you with the tools and inspiration you need to find encouragement in the LORD. As we journey together through the principles found in David's example, you will learn how to shift your focus from the problems that surround you to the God who sustains you. You will discover that no matter what life throws at you, there is always hope in the LORD, and by encouraging yourself in Him, you can face any situation with renewed strength and confidence. This is not just a book about surviving difficult times, but about thriving through them by finding your hope and encouragement in the unchanging character of God. So, whether you are struggling with personal challenges, feeling weighed down by the burdens of life, or simply seeking a deeper sense of peace and purpose, "Renewed Hope-How to Find Encouragement in God" is here to remind you that you are not alone, and that with God, there is always a reason to hope. Let David's example inspire you to turn to the LORD, to find your strength in Him, and to walk forward with a renewed sense of hope, no matter what you face.